How To Collect

SPORTS CARDS

FOR FUN & PROFIT

Paul White

Table of Contents

- Score Sports Cards

- Donruss Sports Cards

- Football Cards

- 2001 Upper Deck Golf Card Set

- About the Author

Introduction
HOW TO COLLECT SPORTS CARDS
For Fun & Profit

I have never grown tired of opening packages of sports cards. I enjoy the thrill of expectantly waiting to see what "cool" cards are waiting for me in the packs that I am about to open.

Every year I would eagerly await the arrival of the first packages of sports cards at our neighbourhood variety store. (My wife's comment to this sentence is probably, "Some things never change!")

I have collected sports cards, especially baseball and hockey cards, since I was eight years old.

I continued to collect cards as a teenager in high school. And, when I enrolled in University, I still found time to open packages of hockey cards each year.

A few years after graduating from university my perspective about collecting baseball and hockey cards changed dramatically. I was no longer concerned about completing each year's set of cards. I still hoped to find the cards of players from my favorite team. But now, I had another goal as I opened packages of cards. I hoped to find a rookie card, especially the first card of the player who was projected to be the next Wayne Gretzky or Nolan Ryan. You see, I had become a sports card dealer!

I had taken my hobby to another level. Oh, I still collected cards that I put into binders and cherished them either because they played for my favorite team, or they were from my hometown area, but now the financial possibilities from selling sports cards were also very appealing.

(Just don't ask me to sell my 1954-55 Topps Alex Delvecchio hockey card; my Steve Yzerman rookie card; or my Eddie Mathews' Red Man Tobacco card!)

I started selling sports cards in 1988. Gradually, through buying and trading cards, I built up my inventory and became a regular dealer on the sportscard show circuit.

During the next 5 or 6 years I not only sold cards but I also studied as many aspects of this hobby/business as I could. I wanted to know as much as possible about this great hobby. Before long, I was being asked by customers and other dealers for appraisal advice.

Today, I still sell cards but I no longer have my own store and I do not attend as many hobby shows as I once did. Collecting sports cards and selling some of them fits nicely with my other career. I am a writer. I like history, hockey, and I love biography. So naturally I have written several hockey biographies and there are more to come.

In the pages that follow I will outline for you the best ways to effectively, efficiently and economically collect sports cards. This information will help you whether you are interested in collecting sports cards as a hobby or if you want to become involved in the business aspect of sports cards, either as a dealer or an investor.

Tips to Preserving Sports Cards

Preserving your sports card collection is very important. After all, you want your sports cards to remain in good condition for a long time. After all you have spent money to purchase your sports cards. So whether you view sports card collecting as an investment or a hobby, or both, you want to protect your sports cards.

The proper tools can make preserving your sports card collection an easy process. Below, I have listed the best equipment and environment to ensure that your sports card collection will be preserved in a safe and efficient manner. Whether you view sports card collecting as an investment, or as a hobby, you will want your sports cards to remain in good condition for a long time.

There are a few things that you can do to protect the condition of your sports card collection.

Storing and Exhibiting Your Sports Card Collection

■ Sports Card Albums or Binders

I like to sit down on a rainy day and look through my sports card albums. I do this not only for pleasure but also to make decisions about upgrading sports cards and double checking player lists to ensure that there are no gaps in the collection.

Finding sports cards to upgrade* your collection is part of the fun of sports card collecting.

*To upgrade your collection involves improving the quality of the sports cards in your collection. Later in the book I will provide more detail about grading your sports cards.

Most of my collection is stored in sports card albums. It is important that your albums or binders are the "D" ring style. These binders have a "D" shape to their rings which allows the binder to be easily closed without "pinching" the pages and thus damaging the contents of the pages.

■ Album or Binder Sheets

The standard sports cards fit into nine-pocket plastic sheets. There are other types of sheets that are available to hold sports cards of different sizes such as the 1964-65 Topps hockey card set also known as the "Tall Boys".

If you have collected sports coins, I suggest that you visit a hobby shop that sells plastic sheets for coin collectors. I use these acid free sheets to hold my hockey or baseball coins in a safe manner that enables me to easily enjoy viewing this valuable and interesting part of my sports memorabilia collection.

Album or binder sheets are one of your most important purchases. There are many different types of plastic sheets available for purchase on the market. But it is important that the plastic sheets that you select are "acid free".

The label will describe the product as "Archives Friendly" or "Acid Free". Do not accept any product that does not say in writing that it is "Acid Free". They will usually be available in better hobby shops, business supply stores, and at hobby shows. If you are unsure of a product ask a store employee about the product before you make the purchase. "Acid Free" sheets will protect your sports cards from deteriorating.

■ **Top-Loaders**

Top-loaders are another way to preserve and store your sports card collection. Once again, make sure that these single cardholders are "Acid Free".

Top loaders are sleeves made of hard, see-through plastic that will hold one sports card. They are usually available in packages of 25 at hobby shows and sports card stores. Sometimes they can be found in the toy department of "big box" stores. But beware of cheaper products in these non-hobby stores as they may not be "Acid Free".

Top-loaders are available in a variety of sizes to fit non-standard sized sports cards such as "Tall-Boy" hockey cards or jersey cards.

■ Sports Card Boxes

Top-loaders need to be stored in boxes. The best sports card storage boxes are designed specifically to hold top-loaders. These boxes usually come in sizes such as 1600 count, often called "shoe-boxes", and 3200 and 5000 count boxes. Make sure the cardboard hobby boxes that you select are also "Acid Free".

Storage Location

Once your collection is placed in the containers of your choice your next sports card preservation decision involves storage location. Where in your home, or elsewhere, are you going to safely keep your collection?

Obviously security is an important consideration when determining where you are going to store your sports memorabilia collection, but the temperature and humidity are equally important circumstances. After all, you want to protect your collection from deteriorating factors.

There are three important physical criteria for the storage location of your sports card collection:

- The temperature of the room must always be in a range between 45-68 degrees F. (8-20 degrees C.)

- The **dampness** of the area should be limited to 45-55 % humidity.

NOTE: With central air conditioning then both the humidity and temperature requirements will be achieved.

- No exposure to direct sunlight.

Handling Sports Cards

When you handle your sports cards try to avoid holding them by the corners. This will reduce the chances of the corners becoming soft or rounded. The best way to hold a card is by the sides (thumb on one side edge and fingers on the edge of the other side of the card) or the top and bottom (thumb on the top and fingers on the bottom edge).

Always make sure that your hands are dry. Some purists recommend the use of cotton gloves such as those used in archives and museums. But, I really don't think that is necessary.

The preservation of your sports card collection is extremely important. After all, you have invested a lot of time and money in your hobby and whether you are collecting for fun or profit you will want to ensure the longevity of your sports card treasures.

The value of old sports cards depends upon some critical information. The physical condition of the card; whether it is a rookie card; if it is a short print; or if it features a Hall of Fame player. The result of your research can mean the difference between a profitable and enjoyable collecting experience and unnecessary expense and disappointment.

Where to Buy Sports Cards
and Other Hobby Materials

When I was a youngster I could buy my hockey and baseball cards at the neighbourhood variety store.

Although some variety stores still carry hockey cards and other sports cards, you cannot usually find a variety of products to choose from. Essentially these stores usually only carry the lower-end products.

If you want to find the more expensive packages of cards or have a wider variety of products to choose from you have a few other options.

First, many of the big box stores carry a wider variety of sports cards. But, again you might be limited to the basic sets provided by the manufacturers. And, these stores may not always re-stock their products. So, your source for purchasing sports cards may dry up before you have been able to collect all the cards that you want or need.

Second, you may live in an area that has a sports card store. Here you will find just about everything you need for your hobby, from cards to the containers necessary to preserve and store your sports cards.

A third venue is a sports card show. Attending a sports card show can be a lot of fun. There are usually many dealers vying for your dollar and you will find a wide variety of products and price ranges to choose from. Consequently, if you take your time and shop around you can save money and often get some great deals on some interesting cards and other sports memorabilia products.

Sports Card Shows

Sports card shows of all sizes offer both educational and entertainment venues for both the new and the experienced sports card collector.

Not only do sports card shows offer the opportunity to purchase cards and products associated with the hobby but they also provide a venue to meet other collectors. This could result in meeting potential sports card trading partners. As well, conversations with dealers and other collectors might help you gather new information about this great hobby.

Types of Sports Card Shows

I have attended many types of sports card shows, both as a vender and as a buyer. Essentially, there are two main types of sports card show, the larger multi-day format shows and the local one-day event. But having defined sports card shows into these two categories is indeed simplistic because these shows can also take on different faces as well. Below I have broadly defined the two main categories of sports card shows:

- **Larger (Multi-Day) Shows**

  The larger shows provide a wider variety of dealers and products. The prices are usually competitive, but not necessarily more competitive than at smaller local shows.

As well as the larger regional sports card shows, there are also trade shows associated with sporting events such as all-star games. These events are sometimes called "Fan Fests" or "Expos".

One of my most memorable sports card show experiences occurred at the "Fan Fest" held in Toronto for the 1991 Major League Baseball All-Star Game. There were sports card dealers and exhibitors from all over North America. The wide array of sport card products and other memorabilia items was truly amazing.

There were many major league baseball players available to sign autographs. The highlight of the entire show for me occurred when I had the opportunity to talk for several minutes with Hall of Fame third baseman Brooks Robinson of the Baltimore Orioles. A baseball featuring Robinson's autograph has a prominent place in my office; a reminder of a meeting with a baseball legend.

Every card collector should try to attend at least one of these major shows. You will not be sorry.

■ Local One Day Sports Card Shows

Local sports card shows provide a new sports card collector with the chance to meet other collectors from the community. Therefore these shows are not only a venue to learn more about the hobby and purchase hobby products, but you could also meet some potential sports card trading partners.

Sports card shows can be an entertaining and educational collecting event. They offer the opportunity for one-stop shopping at a wide range of sports card collectible businesses. Sports card shows also offer the new sports card collector with a chance to meet other collectors and perhaps learn something new about this great hobby.

The best advice that I can offer about a sports card show is to plan ahead and make sure that you have lots of time to spend. Some of my best and most interesting discoveries have occurred while perusing boxes and binders of cards at the tables of various dealers.

And, by taking the time to talk to dealers and other collectors I have continued to learn a lot about this great hobby.

In the next few pages I have provided a checklist of how to prepare for a sports card show. I know it will help both new and veteran collectors increase their enjoyment and productivity while visiting a sports card show.

Preparation for a Sports Card Show

Sports Card Shows

Sports card shows offer many great opportunities for both the new and the experienced sports card collector. To make this experience both rewarding and entertaining I have provided a "checklist" to help you prepare for attending a sports card show.

Preparation for a Sports Card Show "Checklist"

- Make a list of the sports cards and other products that you are looking for at the show and bring this checklist and a pencil to keep track of your trades or purchases. (Entering your list into a spreadsheet or Word document on your computer can make your checklist quick and easy to access and modify.)

- Bring the amount of cash that you will need, because most dealers (especially at smaller shows) are usually not equipped to accept credit cards.

- Pack a cloth bag to carry home your purchases. It will make your visit to the show less cumbersome and awkward.

- Plan to spend at least a couple of hours at the show. If it is a larger show you should give yourself even more time. After all, when you can browse without worrying about the time, it can be a more enjoyable experience. And, as you linger at the tables checking out sports cards and other related products you never know what you might find or the deals you might have otherwise missed!

- If you wear a coat, check it at the coat check before entering the show. The temperatures at some of the venues hosting card shows can get very warm.

- Wear comfortable shoes. Walking and standing for hours on cement floors can really cause back and leg pain, taking the fun out of searching for those elusive singles to fill your check lists.

- Once you arrive at the show walk through the entire show before stopping to purchase. This scouting trip will allow you to see what is available and to get an idea of price ranges. Many of the larger shows offer site maps of the show. This handy map is usually available both at the door and in some cases many show promoters now provide this service on their website.

- Bring one or more card containers to protect your purchases from damage. I usually carry a selection spanning from 50 and 100 count plastic containers to a 400 or 800 count cardboard boxes.

- If you are shopping for vintage sports cards you might consider bringing along "measuring cards". These are a selection of cards representing the different sizes that were available in various years and products. For instance, when I find a card such as 1969-1970 OPC hockey card or a 1962 Topps baseball card that I want for my collection I compare its size to the sample that I have brought along. This allows me to ascertain whether the cards have been "trimmed"*.

*"Trimming" involves carefully pruning the sides of a card to eliminate soft corners, ragged edges or to improve the centering of the sports card. A "trimmed" card has no value on the card market and personally I would avoid a dealer who is selling such cards.

■ If the show features a player signing autographs, bring along cards, photos, pucks, or balls. But check before the show to determine what the player will sign, because not every player will sign everything. Also find out whether there is a difference in cost between getting a card or a hockey puck or a baseball signed. (NB If you are planning to have a sports card signed, you should avoid using a rookie card. Many collectors feel that once a rookie card has been signed it ceases to have the value of a rookie card and assumes only the value of an autograph.)

The best advice that I can offer about a sports card show is to plan ahead and make sure that you have lots of time to spend. Some of my best and most interesting discoveries have occurred while perusing boxes and binders of cards. And, I have learned a lot by just taking the time to talk and listen to the dealers and other collectors that I meet while I am attending sports card shows.

How Much Is My Sports Card Collection Worth?

I am often asked how one can ascertain what their sports card collection is worth.

One of the great things about collecting sports cards is that the value of a card is essentially in the eye of the beholder! This is especially true if you are a sports card collector simply for the love of the hobby.

But, if you consider your sports card collection primarily as an investment, then you will want to know the monetary value of your sports card collection as well as the value of any future trades or purchases aimed at increasing the value of your investment.

Valuing Sports Cards

Your favorite player's card might only carry the value of a common card worth from 10 to 25 cents. But to you it could be as valuable as the card of a player that costs one hundred dollars!

The physical condition of a card is of primary importance when one is determining whether a sports card is priced at; above; or below book value.

Book value is the price set out in a sports card price guide. Although there are a few price guides produced for the hobby, the most respected and widely-used are the price guides produced by the **Beckett Price Guide** company.

If you are trading, buying or selling sports cards you will have an advantage if you know how to determine the physical quality of sports cards.

Grading Sports Cards

There are several grades of condition for sports cards. Although these grades are generally accepted throughout the hobby I have provided the criteria used by Beckett price guides:

- **Mint** (MT): This means that the card is essentially perfect. The four corners are sharp and perfect. The edges are straight and smooth. The colors are sharp and in focus with no print spots or other imperfections. The centering is perfect. (Beckett price guides allow for no worse than 55/45 centering.)

- **Near Mint-Mint** (NRMT-MT): This rating is garnered by a card that features the attributes of a mint card except that the centering must be better than 60/40 and one minor flaw is allowed. This defect could be slight wearing on one corner. Color spots or focus imperfections that are barely noticeable.

- **Near Mint** (NM): The card is centered in a range of 70/30 to 60/40. The sports card has one minor flaw, which could be slight wearing of two or three corners or slightly rough edges. The picture could also have minor print spots or imperfections pertaining to color or focus.

- **Excellent-Mint** (EXMT): The centering is at least 80/20. An EXMT card can have two minor flaws such as two to three fuzzy corners, slightly rough edges and the picture might have print spots, be out of focus or have minor discolorations.

- **Excellent** (EX): Once again 80/20 centering is the maximum allowed. All four corners are fuzzy. Rough edges, border discoloration, focus and color imperfections and minor spots are all considerations.

- **Very Good** (VG): Shows that it has been handled but not abused with slightly rounded corners. The edges may be showing some notching. Color issues on the border and the picture and a loss of gloss are among the telltale signs of a VG card. Hairline creases can be found as well.

- **Good** (G), **Fair** (F) **Poor** (P). These three grades feature significant problems in all categories including serious creases. The degree of degradation I suggest is up to you and whether it is (G), (F) or

(P) is not really important. The only reason you might add a sports card of any of these three grades would be that you needed it to fill a set or it was so rare that you felt that you might never see another card in better condition.

Using these criteria provided by Beckett price guides, you can generally decide how to value your card.

Condition Sensitive

Some individual sports cards as well as complete sets of sports cards command higher values because they are considered "Condition Sensitive".

"Condition Sensitive" is usually the result of two factors.

- Individual sports cards can be tagged as "Condition Sensitive". A good example of this circumstance occurs with the first and last cards of sets produced in the 1950s and 1960s.

   The reason for this special pricing circumstance arose because during the era, young collectors often put their baseball and hockey cards in numerical order and then put an elastic band around the stack of cards. The elastic often cut into the edges of the cards on the top and bottom of the pile, thus making it difficult for modern-day collectors to find the first and last cards in sets from that era in Mint condition.

■ Sometimes the term "Condition Sensitive" is applied to a specific set of sports cards. For instance the 1979-80 OPC and Topps hockey card sets have solid blue borders which tend to chip and fray over time, making it difficult to find mint cards from that year. Ironically, this set contains one of the most sought-after hockey cards, the Wayne Gretzky rookie card!

One of my favorite sets of baseball cards, the 1962 Topps set, with its wood grain finish, is also susceptible to chipping and fraying along the edges.

CAUTION: If the edges of a card from a "Condition Sensitive" set look too good, the sports card may have been "trimmed". To avoid buying a virtually worthless card that has been trimmed, always carry a sample card from the card sets in question to compare the size of the cards.

Sports Card Grading Services

Sports Card Grading Services are rapidly becoming an important part of the sports collecting hobby. This is especially true for those individuals who view their collections as an investment.

Sports card grading has always been a part of the hobby. But, in the past few years, professional grading services have become an increasingly integral part of the sports card collecting hobby.

Reasons for using a Professional Grading Service

Although price guide companies have provided general guidelines about grading conditions (i.e. mint, near mint, etc), the sports card collecting hobby has lacked a formal system of evaluating sports cards. Therefore sports card grading has lacked the objectivity of some other collecting hobbies.

Traditionally, the seller and/or the buyer determined the grade and the corresponding value of a sports card. This circumstance created a lot of room for differences of opinion, not to mention variations in selling prices.

When an objective third party grades sports cards, more merit can be given to their actual value. This circumstance has given rise to the professional sports card grading service industry.

Problems with the Current System of Professional Grading Services

There are an ever-increasing number of grading companies offering their services to sports card collectors. This can leave the collector wondering who to select to grade their cards. Until there is a formalized system of "grading the graders", it is wise to find out as much as you can about the grading service. After all, you are spending the money to have your sports cards evaluated and you want to be able to trust the results that you receive.

Solutions

Here are some ideas to help you make a more informed decision about selecting a sports card grading service.

- Talk to other collectors to find out what they have heard or experienced.

- Talk to dealers to discover what their experience has been with either cards from grading services or grading services themselves.

- Check out hobby magazines and websites for news stories about grading services. However, be careful of stories telling about the great selling prices received for graded cards. These "reports" could really be "advertorials". (Advertisements posing as news stories.)

- Investigate auction sales results and find out which grading products seem to be getting the most attention from sports card buyers.

- Check out the various grading card companies by reading their literature and visiting their websites. Some grading services set up displays and exhibits at sports card shows. If they are offering a "Show Special", bring along a card to be graded.

- Compare all of these sources and then make your own decision.

Benefits of Professional Grading Services

- The important cards in your sports card collection will have an objective evaluation.

- Professionally graded sports cards seem to achieve very high selling prices. Prior to the arrival of this service to the hobby, a group led by hockey superstar Wayne Gretzky purchased a Honus Wagner T-206 baseball card for around $400,000. Since that historic purchase, a "graded" Honus Wagner T-206 sold for more than a million dollars.

A few years ago **Beckett Hockey** magazine reported that a graded Wayne Gretzky rookie card sold for $80,000. This is an amazing amount of money for this hockey card, when one considers that the price guide lists the value of the Gretzky rookie card at about $1,000.00!

With some careful preparation and research, choosing the right sports card grading service can produce some very profitable results.

CAUTION

Because grading services charge a fee for each card, make sure that the value assessed to the card will enable you to make a profit after the sale of the card. Therefore I would not recommend grading cards that are listed in the price guide at a price less than $25.00.

Sports Card Grading Process

Have you ever wondered how sports card grading companies determine a rating for a sports card?

There are several factors that are considered before a decision about the proper grade for a sports card is ascertained.

These factors include:

■ **Size**

Perhaps the easiest factor to determine about a sports card is its size. The sports card is either measured or compared to another card from the same set. This process reveals whether the card has been trimmed.

Although this is a relatively easy procedure the results can have a major impact on the grade of the sports card. If the card is smaller than normal, it probably means that someone has trimmed the edges to reduce soft corners or to eliminate rough edges. Trimming is also used to improve the centering of the card.

■ Weight

I am told that many sports card grading service companies also weigh sports cards. The weight of a card could reveal counterfeiting unless the fake cards were created using paper of the same weight as the original sports card. I am unsure how accurate or widely used this process is.

■ Appearance

The picture on the sports card is examined for clarity and color. Fading of the image and the color of the card are part of this examination. Once again steps are taken to ensure that the sports card is not a counterfeit.

The sports card is given an extensive visual examination looking for minute creases or evidence that someone has "touched up" the finish on the card.

This process is not limited to the front of the card, but the back is scrutinized as well.

The Final Score

After the grading process is complete, a number from 1 to 10 is assigned to the card to designate the grade of the card. The numerical scale runs from 1 (poor) to 10 (gem mint).

It is important to note that a card receiving a "10" grade, will often attract a selling price which by far exceeds the mint price listed in a price guide.

Most professional grading services put the graded card into a sealed plastic container. This container is made of "acid free" material to protect the card from future deterioration.

And, it prohibits someone from switching cards after the carding process is complete.

The entire grading process is in reality, similar to what an experienced collector does every time he or she considers purchasing a sports card for their collection.

Cleaning Your Sports Cards

Cleaning your sports cards is not usually practical or necessary. And, some might even suggest that it is not ethical. Therefore, I only recommend cleaning your sports cards in very rare circumstances.

First of all, I do not believe that you should do anything that alters the physical appearance or condition of a sports card. But there are some circumstances that may warrant some form of cleaning.

- **Dust and Dirt**:

    Simply use a tissue and gently wipe the offending material from the card.

- **Wax Stains**:
    Sports cards that were packaged in wax packs (Pre-1990 era) sometimes have some wax on the card that was next to where the pack was sealed.

After years of trial and error, I have discovered a safe and effective way to remove wax stains.

Solution: Take a sheet or two of thick quilted paper towels and fold them over twice. Cover the folded paper towel with one layer of "silky" nylon stockings. Hold the sports card in one hand and gently rub the wax-stained area with stocking-covered paper towel.

CAUTION: Never apply water to clean any sports card. This is especially true of some of the early Parkhurst hockey cards. The paint seems to have been water-soluble. I know one collector who has what was once a gem-mint Henri Richard card with a strip down the front showing bare cardboard!

■ **Bubble Gum**:

When you open a package of older O.P.C. or Topps hockey and baseball cards you might find bubble gum stuck to a card. Personally, I have never been able to successfully remove the gum from the card without ruining the card.

Freezer Method: Fact or Fiction?

A few collectors claim that they have successfully removed gum from a sports card by putting the card into their refrigerator freezer for a few hours. When they take the card out of the deep freeze; the gum simply falls away after a couple of gentle taps. It might be worth a try, but I can't verify it.

I do not try to clean my sports cards. The possibility of damage is too great. Besides, most purists would claim that you are risking altering the condition of the card. But, as I have pointed out above there are a couple of exceptions to the rule.

Sports Card Collecting Resources:
The Internet

The Internet has made the gathering of information much easier and more efficient. The hobby of sports card collecting is no different.

If you want find out the location of the sports card stores or upcoming sports card shows in a certain geographic area all you have to do is log on to the Internet and you are only a few clicks away from finding what you are seeking.

All of the sports card companies have their own websites. Here you can find product information such as release dates, etc. If you collect sets, some sports card manufacturers provide checklists of the products that they have produced.

Price Guides such as Beckett Publications also have their own websites. These sites promote their products and services. One service that I really appreciate is their "Show Listings". With a couple of clicks of the mouse I can find the dates and locations of upcoming sports card shows. This is especially helpful when I am traveling.

Also, there are more and more websites and blogs which offer commentary and reviews of sports card sets. Many of them offer a forum for debate and questions about sports cards, players, and teams etc.

Researching players is an important aspect of sports card collecting. Tracking players' statistics and keeping up to date about trades are also extremely helpful to collectors. There are many sources on the Internet to help you find this information.

My first stop on any research project is the website of the various leagues such as mlb.com, nhl.com, nfl.com, pga.com and nascar.com.

Media sites are extremely important for finding the latest news and rumours in major league sports. For instance, if you are a golf card collector, one of my favorite sites is www.golfchannel.com. This site has up-to-date statistics and great stories about golf. I also rely a lot on www.espn.com for a broader range of sports news.

Another big advantage that the web offers the sports card researcher is access to local newspapers anywhere in the world. Consequently, you can always be up-to-date on all of the latest necessary to stay on top of your hobby.

And last, and certainly not the least, the Internet allows you to connect with other collectors to buy, sell or trade sports cards. This aspect of the hobby goes far beyond E-Bay. There are a wide range of collector clubs and other forms of trading venues that you can access.

Collecting Sports Card Sets

Collecting sports cards has been my passion for many years. Like many collectors each new set meant the beginning of a quest to collect the entire set of cards each year.

Today many people still collect the sets of cards produced each year by the sports card manufacturers. However, the growth of the sports card industry has meant a corresponding increase in the number of products produced each year. To try to collect every set created each season is very time consuming and can be very expensive. But there are some alternative collecting practices to consider.

1/ Collect the set produced by the same company every year. Once you have collected the current edition you can try to build sets manufactured by that company in previous years. For instance I know of several collectors who have spent many years putting together complete sets of every Topps baseball cards since the first set was introduced in 1951. This can seem to be a never-ending project but the quest to find those elusive "last cards" to complete a set can be an exciting project.

But, once a set is complete it does not always mean that their search is over. A critical evaluation of a completed set, especially one that is many decades old could reveal that not all the cards are in great shape. So, a new quest begins. Now, the collector may choose to try and find better quality cards to upgrade some of the cards.

The beauty of this type of set collecting is that you can set the parameters of your collecting. Financial considerations may dictate that your sets may contain cards that are less than pristine. But, nevertheless, you still have collected and completed the entire set!

2/ Another set building process could involve checking out the new product produced each season selecting the one that you like best. After all, the sports card manufacturers produce several great products each year. All you have to do is buy a few packs and decide which set you want to build that season.

Creating and Collecting Your Own
Sports Card Subsets

Creating and collecting you own sports card sets can be a lot of fun. But with the large variety of products available on today's sports card market this can be an expensive project. But there are alternative ways to collect sports cards. Here are few ideas for your consideration:

- **Favorite team**: I used to collect several sets every year but in the past few years I have started to put together a collection of cards for the players from my favorite hockey and baseball teams, the Detroit Red Wings, the Tampa Lightning and the Milwaukee Braves.

Finding Milwaukee Braves' cards means that I have to attend sports card shows which feature vintage baseball card dealers. While the Red Wings collection involves vintage sports cards, I can also have the fun of opening packs of hockey cards each season to try and find the newest cards featuring my hockey team.

■ **Favorite players**: Some collectors limit their collections to only those of their favorite players. When I was a youngster I collected as many cards of my favorite player as I possibly could. However, there is a downside to such fanaticism. Because I hated the New York Yankees I traded away every one of their cards that came into my possession. Alas, I now have boxes of cards of Milwaukee Braves cards and nowhere in my collection is there one Mickey Mantle card!

■ **Favorite position player**: This is a great way to build a unique collection. If you were a second baseman in baseball or tight end in football, building a collection of second basemen or tight ends can be an entertaining hobby. I know a few collectors who collect every goalie card that they can find. One of these collections contains more than 17,000 different cards!

- **Hometown Team or Players**: This type of collection can take two very distinct routes. Collecting the cards of players who grew up in your hometown can be very special, especially if they were your team mate when you played local minor sports.

If you live in the vicinity of a major league team, then collecting their cards can be a great way to express your fan loyalty. However, be aware that card dealers often sell local cards at a premium.

I often take advantage of hometown premium pricing. For instance if I am going to the Tampa area, I might take along some extra Steven Stamkos hockey cards in hopes of trading for some Detroit Red Wings or Milwaukee Brave cards at a local card show or card shop.

- **Rookie cards**: Probably the most popular form of specialty sports card collecting is amassing rookie cards for as many players as possible. Usually a rookie card collector has an eye towards sports cards as an investment because a player's rookie card is priced according to his success on the ice or the playing field. Consequently, a Sidney Crosby or Derek Jeter rookie card is going to cost considerably more than the rookie card of a fringe player.

- **Vintage Cards** (pre-1980): Some collectors have turned to collecting vintage sports cards. There are probably a few reasons why they find vintage cards fun to collect. First they are usually harder to find and carry a higher price tag. Because there are fewer cards from this era their price has likely been established and is not subject to the whims of the market like the cards of current players.

Secondly, these cards offer a look at the early days of sports. Personally, I like the vintage cards because their design and colors which were created without the aid of modern graphic design equipment and techniques. For instance two of my favorite sets are the 1954-55 Topps hockey set (For a and the 1954 Topps baseball sets. But another set the 1971-72 OPC hockey card set features two of the nicest cards ever produced, the farewell tribute cards for Jean Beliveau and Gordie Howe.

- **Unique cards**: Collecting sports cards is a very subjective hobby. This is especially true when it comes to unique sports cards. What may be unique to you may seem quite ordinary to someone else. For instance, I like to collect sports cards that come in food products. This can mean anything from sports cards that are part of a promotion at a restaurant chain to cards found on the back of cereal boxes or in the lids of peanut butter jars.

- **Error and variation cards**: As the title suggests error cards can simply mean that some mistake was made during the production of the card. Two of the more famous error cards featured Atlanta Braves star Dale Murphy and former Montreal Canadiens legend Jacques Lemaire.

The Dale Murphy reverse negative card in the 1989 Upper Deck Baseball card set is probably one of the main reasons why collectors started building error and variation subsets in their sports card collections. (Why did the Murphy card help to spawn the rise of collectors or errors and variations cards? I think that it was combination of two factors. One the fascination with the arrival of Upper Deck cards with their various innovations to the hobby. And, secondly, the sports card collecting hobby was expanding in unprecedented numbers. With the increasing number of collectors there was simply bound to be a growth in ideas about collectibles.

The 1974-1975 OPC hockey card of Hall of Fame player and NHL coach Jacques Lemaire has always been considered an oddity in the industry. This hockey card shows the Montreal Canadiens star wearing the jersey and is listed as a member of a team that he never played for, the Buffalo Sabres.

How did Lemaire's hockey card end up with him wearing a Sabres uniform? The answer lies in the technique used by card companies in the 1970s. A few different players were photographed in various formats (action photo or simply pictures of the player featuring his head and shoulders). Then heads and team jerseys were superimposed on these basic photos. Whoever performed this operation on the Lemaire hockey card either did not know that he played for the Canadiens or he simply made a mistake.

- **Notorious cards**: This is an incredibly subjective category because what might be notorious to some may not be to others. The card that comes to mind immediately is the 1989 Fleer baseball card of Billy Ripken. This card featured a very uncomplimentary comment printed on the knob of Ripken's baseball bat. Fleer tried several means of removing the two-word phrase. Each version appeared as a "corrected" card.

The limits to the subsets that can be created are only bounded by the constraints of your imagination. The most important rule of any hobby, enjoy!

Rookie Cards and Inserts

Rookie Cards

A rookie card is a player's first major league sports card.

If you are considering sports card collecting as an investment vehicle, then rookie cards should be high on your list.

Consequently, rookie cards are one of the most highly prized types of cards for many sport card collectors.

Determining the Value of Rookie Cards

A player can have several different rookie cards. Each sports card set produced in the same year can contain a rookie card of a specific player. But this does not mean that all the rookie cards for the same player will have the same value.

Factors Determining the Value of Rookie Cards:

- **Print Run**

The print run of a set of cards is a major determining factor in the price of any sports card and especially the value of rookie cards. The fewer cards produced, the higher the hobby value. A good example of how the production numbers impact on hobby prices is illustrated by the prices of rookie cards that were produced in the early 1990s.

During that era of the sports card collecting industry, companies produced massive numbers of cards. Consequently, the sports cards of that period do not enjoy high ranking in the hobby.

The rookie card for Detroit Red Wings star defenseman Nicklas Lidstrom is a good example of this situation. Lidstrom is probably the greatest defenseman in the history of the NHL whose name is not Bobby Orr. Yet his rookie cards can be purchased for less than $5.00! (The price guides list Lidstrom's 1991-92 Upper Deck rookie card to be worth around $2.50.)

■ Regional Favorites

Regional favouritism is also a large factor in the price of a rookie card. Obviously local heroes command premium prices. I often take advantage of this phenomenon. When I travel I take rookie cards of local heroes and trade for cards that I need for my collection.

There is a downside to buying a hometown favorite. Be prepared for the fact when this player leaves town for another team, either by trade or free agency, the premium that you paid or expected to receive when you sold this card more than likely will disappear.

■ High Expectations

Sometimes a new player enters the big leagues surrounded by hype and attention. The sports card hobby pays attention to this type of activity. Consequently, some rookie cards start out valued in the hundreds of dollars before the player has even completed his first big league season.

Hobbyists should always be wary of over-hyped rookies and their rookie cards. After all, you only have to consider the hype around Eric Lindros when he was about to play in the NHL. Today, his once highly-prized Score rookie card lists around $3.00 and frankly, you can probably buy it for considerably less!

Why Keep Rookie Cards?

It is important to remember that although some cards lose their rookie card lustre and their hobby price drops, there are other rookie cards that follow the opposite path.

Just because a rookie card languishes in the common card price range, it does not mean that one day its value will not dramatically increase. A classic example of this situation is the rookie card of Calgary Flames goaltender Miikka Kiprusoff. His rookie card #125 in the 1994-1995 Finest set was virtually unwanted and unnoticed for years.

What happened to spike the interest and the price? First, he won a Vezina Trophy as the top goaltender in the National

Hockey League. But, even more importantly he carried the Flames to the Stanley Cup Finals. Despite the fact that his team ultimately lost the championship to the Tampa Lightning, his seven-game appearance on national television in both Canada and the United States garnered him huge hobby attention. Now, Kiprusoff's rookie card that once sold as a common card soared in the price guides to around $25.00! If you had saved a few of these cards when they were first valued at less than a dollar, you would have made a tidy profit!

Ultimate Rookie Cards

Although there are many reasons for collecting rookie cards the goal is to find what I call the Ultimate Rookie Card. What is the Ultimate Rookie Card? I will answer with three names, Bobby Orr, Wayne Gretzky, and Sidney Crosby! Whenever anyone buys the rookie card of a highly touted rookie, their dream is that it will become the next "Big One". Obviously, it does not happen very often. But that is the stuff that makes sport card collectors' dream!

Minor League & Amateur League Sports Cards

Although some minor leagues have from time-to-time produced complete sets of cards representing players from every team in their league, the usual circumstance is that teams produce their own sets of cards.

These team sets from leagues such as minor league baseball and junior hockey are a great sports card collectible.

Minor League Baseball Team Sets

The cards in minor league sets do not often dramatically increase in price. But regardless of the possible monetary return, minor league baseball team sets can perhaps provide another unique aspect to your sports card collection.

When I go on a vacation, I often attend minor league baseball games. It was on a holiday in 1988 that I purchased my first minor league baseball team set. I was driving along I-4 in Florida, just west of Orlando when I noticed a highway sign pointing to Baseball City. I had to stop and check it out.

I soon discovered that this was the minor league complex of the Kansas City Royals' organization and the home of the Baseball City Royals of the Florida State League. The team was playing its first season at this location and they would continue to play at this great baseball facility until the end of the 1992 baseball season.

At the stadium store, I purchased the team set of baseball cards for $5.00.

The set, produced by Star, consisted of 25 numbered cards. The backs gave great descriptions of each player's background including when they had been drafted into the Royals' organization.

At that point in time, only one player in the set was recognizable to me. His name was Brian McRae, the son of major league player, Hal McRae.

But after more than two decades a look at the team set reveals more than a half a dozen players who played in the big leagues. Besides Brian McRae, two others in that minor baseball team set stand out.

In 1988, Kevin Appier was in his second season of professional baseball. The other player was drafted in the 58th round of the June 1987 Amateur Draft. But despite his very late round draft selection, Jeff Conine enjoyed a lengthy career in major league baseball, including two trips to the World Series.

NOTE: Remember, that minor league sets do not contain rookie cards. The only sports cards to qualify as a rookie card are those manufactured on a national, or international, scale and by the sports card companies licensed to print cards for MLB, the NHL, NFL and NBA.

Minor League Baseball Sets are a nice addition to any sports card collection, but for me they are also a reminder of my past vacation experiences!

Junior Hockey Card Sets

Team sets can be found in many different locations and in the arenas and stadiums of teams playing in many levels of professional and amateur sport. A trip to an NHL game will usually find the home team's set of cards for sale at the various concession booths around the stadium.

When I travel to a junior hockey game, I often check to see if the home team has produced a set of hockey cards featuring their players. Over the years I have discovered some great hockey card teams sets that are truly unique. For instance, a few years ago while attending an Owen Sound Attack OHL game I was able to purchase a 2003-04 team set that just about the entire team had individually autographed. They were not copied autographs. Many of the players had sat down and signed each hockey card!

Needless to say, this set of hockey cards has a place in my collection. After all, there were some signed cards of players who had gone on to careers in professional hockey, including super star Bobby Ryan, who had been selected

2nd overall in the NHL Entry Draft. The player who was chosen 1st overall that year was non other than Sidney Crosby.

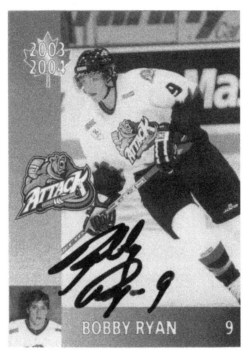

But there were more interesting autographed hockey cards. Card #7 featured defenseman Mark Giordano, who became the captain of the Calgary Flames. (I have included below a signed hockey card for Giordano from the 2002-03 team set.) Other players who made it to the NHL, some for only a short-lived career, included Brad Richardson, Stefan Ruzicka, Dan LaCosta and Mike Angelidis.

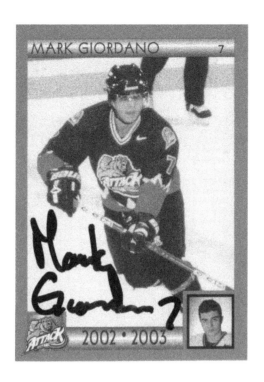

These set of hockey cards that I had autographed turned me into a collector of junior hockey cards.

What makes junior hockey team sets so attractive to hockey card collectors? First, they are usually printed for a limited selling region. Therefore the print runs are small. Second, because they are usually produced by a local company the design and layout of the cards may be unique. And, finally the price is often very affordable often ranging between five and ten dollars for the complete set.

You just never know which players will go on to the NHL.

Above, I have posted the hockey card of Ottawa 67s Petr
Mrazek. This star goaltender from the Ontario Hockey
League has become a goaltending prospect for the Detroit
Red Wings.

Sports Cards History

Why should you know about the history of sports cards?

First, collectors and future collectors should know that sports cards are not a recent innovation. And secondly, knowing about some of the earlier productions of sports cards might provide some ideas about expanding your collectibles hobby.

The first sports cards appeared in the 1860s as an advertising medium.

Sports cards have a long and varied history. Sports cards were originally produced as an advertising vehicle to attract consumers to purchase products such as breakfast cereal and sporting goods. Ironically, we often consider sports cards as being created to attract youngsters. But they also have been used to promote the purchase of a broad range of commodities for adults including cigars and cigarettes. It is only in the last two or three decades that sports cards have become a commercial industry unto themselves.

For instance, in 1868, Peck and Snyder, a New York sporting goods store, produced cards featuring pictures of baseball teams on one side and advertisements for products sold in their store on the other side of the card.

Tobacco Cards

Cards·featuring sports teams and athletes have continued to appear as advertising tools for products and companies since the mid-1800s. But, in the 1880s, sports cards entered a new phase in their evolution.

This next stage occurred, when perhaps for the first time, sports cards were inserted inside packaging of another product. In the 1880s, tobacco manufacturers put baseball cards inside cigarette and other tobacco packages.

Within a decade, sports cards featuring other sports such as football and boxing were also inserted inside tobacco product packaging.

Perhaps the most famous sports card ever produced was a tobacco card. This baseball card featured one of the early superstars of that sport, Honus Wagner.

However, Wagner was opposed to smoking. Consequently he was opposed to the idea of his image being used to sell tobacco products. He demanded that his card be removed from production.

Fearing Wagner's threat of litigation, the company complied and further production runs never occurred. However, some of the Wagner cards that had been produced were already in circulation. The limited number, the story about why production was halted, and of course Wagner's superstar status in baseball history has led to high prices for those remaining cards. The Wagner T-206 card gained even more recognition when a group of investors led by hockey superstar Wayne Gretzky spent more than $400,000 to purchase a Honus Wagner T-206.

In the 1950s Red Man Tobacco produced several runs of cards. In fact, one of my favorite cards is a 1954 Red Man

Tobacco card of Eddie Mathews the Hall of Fame third baseman for the Milwaukee Braves.

Perhaps the last time that tobacco products and sports cards were linked occurred in 1962-1963 when El Producto Cigars created a set of six circular shaped cards featuring National Hockey League stars. Another feature of this unique little set of hockey cards is their colors. The brightness and texture of these cards were spectacular for an era that predates digital printing. Because these hockey cards are very rare, don't expect to find them in the "commons" bin at your neighborhood sports card store or at a card show.

The set of El Producto hockey cards was headlined by the greatest player of that era, Gordie Howe who was featured as card #3 in the set. The other five included card #1 Jean Beliveau, #2 Glenn Hall, #4 Dave Keon, #5 Frank Mahovlich and #6 Henri Richard.

At this point in history, perhaps due to social pressures about the impact of tobacco products on health, tobacco companies ceased to produce any more sports card products.

Candy and Bubble Gum Cards

In the early 1900s candy companies entered the business of producing sports cards.

In an effort to promote their product, Cracker Jacks inserted baseball cards into their boxes. The 1914 Cracker Jack Baseball set features 144 cards of the stars of the era. The 1915 edition of Cracker Jack Baseball cards was expanded to include 176 cards.

In the 1920s candy bar companies in Canada produced hockey cards such as the 1923 Paulin's Candy hockey cards and the 1924 Maple Crispette hockey cards.

The 1930s marked the beginning of the dominance of bubble gum companies as distributors of sports cards. In 1933 the Goudey Gum Company produced a set of 239 cards. Baseball cards were produced up until the Second

World War. And, in 1933 the O-Pee-Chee company of London Ontario produced its first set of hockey cards.

Play Ball Cards

Although there were some minor incursions into the sports card world during the Second World War it was not until after the war that sports cards as we know them today really took a hold on North American society. And, once again it was bubble gum companies that led the industry.

In 1948 Bowman Gum and the Leaf Candy Company issued baseball cards.

In 1951, the Topps Bubble gum Company issued two small sets, Topps Blue Backs and Topps Red Backs baseball cards.

Topps began its domination of the industry with a 407 card set in 1952. This is perhaps the most famous Topps baseball set of all-time because it contains the most expensive baseball rookie card of the modern era, the legendary Mickey Mantle Rookie Card.

Hockey cards appeared on the shelves of variety stores in 1951. The 1951-52 Parkhurst hockey card set is unique for a couple of reasons. First of all, the cards are about half the size of hockey cards that are produced today. This was the only year that the smaller version of a hockey card appeared. The year after the initial Parkhurst hockey set, and since, with only a few exceptions hockey cards have been produced in the more traditional size.

The second unique aspect of the 1951-52 set is the fact that about 80% of the cards appearing in the set are rookie cards. And what a roster of rookie cards can be found in this little set!

HY BULLER —New York Rangers
Playing Position—Defense
Born: Montreal, Que., Mar. 15, 1926
No. 91 in the "PARKIE" 1951-52 Hockey Series.

Detroit Red Wing superstar Gordie Howe's first hockey card tops the list. But Howe is not the only legend in this set, Rocket Richard, goaltending great Terry Sawchuk and many more Hall of Fame players can be found depicted in this unique inaugural hockey card set. For a hockey historian or just a super hockey fan this set is a "must have" part of your collection!

In 1954, the Topps Company of Brooklyn New York produced its first hockey card set. A few years earlier Topps had started producing baseball cards. So it was probably only natural that this company would start producing hockey cards.

The 1954-55 Topps hockey card set is one of my personal favourites! And, the cards are a little bigger in physical size than traditional hockey cards. The set only features the four American-based teams, Detroit, Boston, Chicago and New York. (For the next few years, Topps and Parkhurst would split the teams. For instance, most often Parkhurst would produce cards depicting Toronto, Montreal and Detroit and the Topps company would print players from the other three teams.)

The 1968-69 hockey season, marked the return of O-Pee-Chee to the hockey card market. The London Ontario based company had produced sets of hockey cards in the 1930s but had been forced to take a hiatus because of World War Two. For whatever reason, O-Pee-Chee did not return to the business of hockey cards until 1968.

Perhaps, O-Pee-Chee's return was precipitated by the fact that in 1964 Parkhurst ceased production of hockey cards and for four years the market was the sole domain of Topps. (Parkhurst hockey cards would return to the hockey card industry, producing its first hockey set in more than two-and-half decades in 1991.)

Together, Topps and O-Pee-Chee, would produce hockey cards until 1990-91, when a new company, Upper Deck, entered the market with an impact that would change the face of the collectibles' industry forever.

There were other companies who, almost simultaneously, with Upper Deck's entrance on the hockey scene, who threw their hats into the ring that would become the sports card industry. These included three companies who had produced baseball cards in the 1980s, Fleer, Score and Donruss; and two hockey companies Parkhurst and Pro-Set. (Pro-Set would produce a golf sports card set almost at the same time as their inaugural hockey card set arrived on the sports collecting scene.)

Not to be outdone by the innovations of these new companies, O-Pee-Chee and Topps created a top-of-the-line product called Premier.

Today, a considerable number of the sports card labels remain. But, many of them are owned by the same company, Upper Deck. And, more recently, another player has entered the hockey card market. Panini who had long been known as manufacturer of hockey stickers in 2010 began producing regular-sized hockey cards.

In January 2009, Panini acquired an exclusive license to produce NBA trading cards and stickers effective with the 2009-10 NBA season. On March 13, 2009, Panini acquired the Texas-based trading card manufacturer Donruss Playoff LP. This acquisition also gave Panini the NFL and NFLPA licenses owned by Donruss.

In March 2010, Panini expanded its portfolio of licenses when it acquired a license from the NHL and the NHLPA. This move into the world of hockey cards and the release of their first issue of hockey cards for the 2010-11 season, spelled the end of five-year period in which Upper Deck had been the sole manufacturer of hockey cards.

Vintage Sports Card Review:
1954-1955 Topps Hockey Set

I have to admit that the 1954-1955 Topps hockey set is my favorite set of hockey cards.

The 1954-55 set is historically significant because it is the first set of hockey cards produced by Topps. And what a great set it is!

Cards in the Set: 60

Hobby Favorite: Card #8 Gordie Howe

My Favorite: Card #39 Alex Delvecchio

Rookie Cards: 10 rookie cards

Hobby Favorite Rookie Card: Doug Mohns

The front of each of the cards features a colourful artist's rendition of the hockey player on a white background. A large color image of the player's team logo is located in the upper corner of the card. The bottom edge of the card has a two-color banner with the player's name and team in white lettering with his position in black letters.

The biography of the featured player along with his statistics from the previous season can be found on the back of the card.

The 1954-1955 Topps hockey card set features only the cards of the four American-based hockey teams in the National Hockey League at the time. (Detroit Red Wings, Boston Bruins, Chicago Black Hawks and New York Rangers)

Prior to this set, Parkhurst was the only hockey card manufacturer. This Toronto-based company had started printing hockey cards in 1951.

The first card (Dick Gamble) and the last card (Milt Schmidt) in the 1954-55 Topps set are priced as "Condition Sensitive" cards. If you are looking for these cards in mint condition be prepared to pay a premium price.

Note: Most of the first and last cards of baseball and hockey card sets prior to 1980 are priced as "Condition Sensitive". There is an interesting reason why these cards are given this description. It is because during this era the cards were collated from first to last and then the collector, usually a school boy held his stack of cards together with an elastic band. Over time, the elastic band cut into the edges of the top and bottom cards. These were most often the first and last numbered cards.

The roster of players featured in this wonderful set of vintage hockey cards is headlined by Hall of Fame legends Gordie Howe and Terry Sawchuk. There are many other Hall of Fame players in the set. Milt Schmidt's #60 card is the last card in the set and it is also the last player card ever produced of this great Bruins' star and member of the Hockey Hall of Fame.
Every collector of vintage hockey should strive to have at least one card from this outstanding set.

Upper Deck Sports Cards

Upper Deck sports cards arrived on the sports card-collecting scene in 1989 with the launching of the first Upper Deck baseball card set.

When the 1989 Upper Deck baseball cards were first released they presented the hobby with an entirely new product. Although the photography on other products was good, there was something special and unique about pictures featured in the Upper Deck's cards.

Perhaps foreseeing the problems of "pack searching" and counterfeiting, Upper Deck introduced foil packaging and "anti-counterfeiting holograms" to the sports card industry.

The new look and feel Upper Deck baseball cards were an immediate success with collectors. But, it should also be mentioned that the 1989 set's popularity probably was also the result of two other factors.

One factor that impacted on the popularity of this set was the huge number of great rookie cards in 1989 led by the number one card in the set, the rookie card of Ken Griffey Jr.

The other phenomenon that impacted on the huge demand for Upper Deck's first baseball set was the emergence of the error card as a collectible entity in the sports card collecting industry.

Whether by design or error, two cards, one featuring Atlanta Braves' star Dale Murphy and other the card of Detroit Tigers journeyman Pat Sheridan, were printed from reverse negatives producing a backwards image of the players. The prices for these two baseball cards skyrocketed as collectors purchased packages looking for these two cards.

At the same time a new thought-process emerged in the hobby. The existence of two errors meant that there might be more. This created a whole new genre of sports card collector, the "error and variation" specialist. Collectors, especially dealers, started examining sports cards from other companies and from other eras of the industry looking for more "errors and variations".

Upper Deck's success in 1989 led to the emergence of other Upper Deck products. In 1990, the company released its first hockey set and the following year (1991) Upper Deck basketball and football cards made their debut into world of sports card collecting.

Insert Cards

In the 1990s Upper Deck introduced the short printed premium "Insert Card" to the hobby.

Baseball Heroes

The first "Insert Cards" in the 1990 Upper Deck baseball packages featured a nine-card mini-set called "Baseball Heroes". This small subset featured highlights of the career of baseball legend Reggie Jackson.

Although the "Baseball Heroes" cards were only randomly found in packages, Upper Deck also introduced an even more elusive Insert Card in the 1990 baseball set, a limited-edition autograph card signed by Reggie Jackson. There were 2500 autograph cards, each bearing a number from 1 to 2500.

Recognizing the success of the "Baseball Heroes" inserts cards and the autograph cards Upper Deck applied the same process when the company started publishing cards for other sports. Soon the sport card collectors were buying packages of hockey and football cards in order to find "Heroes" cards of superstars like football's Joe Montana and hockey's Wayne Gretzky. And, of the autographs of these popular superstars also were in great demand.

The autographed card as a "short printed" insert created more demand among collectors for packs to crack. To protect the hobbyist and help maintain the value of the autographs the company created Upper Deck Authenticated in 1992. This five-step process helped to guarantee that inserted autograph cards were genuine.

Because of Upper Deck's innovative packaging ideas and the creation of premium-valued insert cards, it was not long before the rest of the industry was creating similar products.

The Upper Deck Company continued to aggressively work to create new sports card collecting products. From its inaugural baseball set in 1989, the company has expanded to produce card sets for every major North American sport. In some sports, like hockey, Upper Deck has developed several other unique sets of cards. And, to even further increase their market share, this California-based company has also purchased some of their competitor companies.

In less than two decades Upper Deck has become a dominant factor in the business of sports cards.

1989 Upper Deck Baseball Card Set

The arrival of the 1989 Upper Deck baseball set ignited a new trend in sports card collecting.

When it was announced that a new company was about to jump into the world of baseball cards, sports card dealers and collectors alike were unsure what the impact would be.

Prior to 1989, the baseball card collecting industry had been almost the exclusive domain of Topps. But, in the previous decade new companies had moved in to challenge Topps' three-decade domination of the baseball card industry. Both Donruss and Fleer started producing baseball cards on an annual basis in 1981.

The previous year, 1988, Score had entered the card wars with a set of baseball cards. Now, there was about to be a new kid on the block.

This new kid, Upper Deck, brought a whole new set of "bells and whistles" to entice the baseball card collector.

Of course, the 1989 Upper Deck baseball set had lots of high-profile rookie cards. But then, so did most of the baseball card products that year. The group of new players led by the sensational Ken Griffey Jr., was outstanding.

Upper Deck's entry into the market went far beyond just producing another traditional set of baseball cards. The company introduced new technology that would provide a dramatic impact on the sport card industry.

The first time one looked at a package of Upper Deck baseball cards the changes in technology were evident. The old style of wax packaging had been replaced with foil wrapping. For the serious collector this was a welcome innovation. Foil packaging made it more difficult to search packs.

The wax packs were easily opened and re-sealed. I had an interesting experience with a dealer who was selling wax packs that he had opened, searched and re-sealed.

At a card show in 1988, I purchased several packages of 1980 Topps baseball cards. As my friends watched, I opened the packs. I had a big surprise when I opened the third pack. In the pack I found baseball cards from 1986 and 1987, as well as a football card!

I immediately returned to the dealer who had sold me the packages and confronted him about searching and re-sealing the packs. With a rather sheepish look on his face he returned my money.

Afterwards, my friends and I had a good laugh about what a stupid criminal he had been! Imagine putting cards from other years and other sports into packages and then trying to sell them!

Needless to say, my friends and I never purchased anything from this vendor. And, we told a lot of other collectors about this dealer's attempt to take advantage of his customers.

The use of holograms provided another safety feature for the sports card collector. This anti-counterfeiting measure would help reduce the number of rookie cards that were being duplicated and bring a further sense of security to those who invested in sports cards.

As if the technological advances were not enough to enhance Upper Deck's position in the sports collectible industry, there was another phenomenon attached to the 1989 baseball set. Error cards became an important component in the demand for these foil-packed cards.

There had always been error cards in the industry. But, perhaps for the first time error cards became an important commodity.

The revelation that the cards of Dale Murphy and Pat Sheridan had been printed from reverse negatives drove the prices of packages of Upper Deck baseball cards to previously unknown high levels. Soon collectors were scouring their card collections for errors. If there were two mistakes then there could be more.

NOTE: It is important to know that some error cards are never corrected. The Price Guides usually mark these cards with "UER" behind the players name to denote "Uncorrected Error". These cards usually do not carry a premium price.

The success of the 1989 Upper Deck baseball set led to the company producing in the next few years hockey, football and basketball card sets. Today, Upper Deck is an important player in the production of most of the major North American sports.

1989 Upper Deck Baseball Set: Quick Facts

Total Number of Cards in the set: 800
Basic Set: 1-700
Extended Set: 701-800

Both the Basic set and Extended Set (also known as High Numbers Set) were available in packages and factory sets.

Hobby Favorite Card: Card #1 - Ken Griffey Jr. Rookie

Score Sports Cards

In 1988, Score baseball cards made their debut in the world of baseball card collecting. However, this was not the first set of baseball cards produced by the company who owned Score. In 1985, Orthographics created a set of "Magic Motion", three-dimensional baseball cards under the name "Sportflics".

The 1988 Score baseball set contained 660 cards. This baseball set featured brightly colored borders and great action photography. The set featured six different colors of borders divided into 110-card units. For instance the baseball cards numbered from 1 to 110 featured magenta colored borders. Each successive 110-card unit was displayed with a different brightly colored border. Each package of baseball cards contained cards from each of the various 110-card units.

The successful reception by collectors spurred the company to expand beyond baseball into other sports. The very next year, 1989, Score Football, kicked off with a highly popular 330–card set, featuring a huge line-up of the rookie cards of some of the top players of the era.

Perhaps it was the great rookie class of 1989 that helped Score Football, but whatever the reason, Score has continually produced top-calibre football sets.

A year later, in 1990, Score skated into the business of hockey cards. The 1990-91 Score hockey card set was one of the most anticipated sets of trading cards for many years. First, collectors were anxious to see if the company could duplicate the success of Score Football. But, perhaps more importantly, collectors and hockey fans alike were eagerly awaiting the appearance of the rookie card of the highly-touted and controversial Eric Lindros.

Score had achieved a major coup, in the hockey card industry, when they signed Lindros to an exclusive contract that limited the appearance of the young superstar's rookie card only to Score trading card products.

The next year, 1991-92 Score added another name to the company's ever-growing list of sports card products. The Pinnacle hockey and baseball cards were considered to be premium sports cards. The Pinnacle brand continued in both sports until 1998. This brand returned to the hockey card market in 2010.

In 1993, the company created another new high-end commodity with Score Select baseball cards. A year later, for the 1994-95 hockey season, Score Select hockey made its debut. This premium brand continued on the market until 1997.

Some of my favorite sports cards are Score products. The company produced some huge baseball sets, the 1991 Score baseball set has a whopping 893 cards and the factory set for that year had 900 cards.

One of the attractions of these Score baseball cards for me was the unique presentation on some of the cards. For instance, the 1991 baseball set features a series of cards with some of the game's star players like Cal Ripken in caricatures.

I still enjoy the Score baseball and hockey cards from the company's formative years that are in my collection and I am always on the lookout for other cards from this company.

Donruss Sports Cards

Although Donruss emerged on the sports card scene in 1981, with sets of baseball cards and golf cards, the company has a much longer history in the trading card industry.

The Donruss company name was created in 1954. This new company came into being when two brothers Donald and Russell Weiner, took ownership of the Thomas Weiner Company, a company that produced bubble gum and candy products.

During the 1950s and 1960s Donruss not only continued manufacturing candy and bubble gum, but also started producing trading cards featuring various aspects of the entertainment industry.

In 1981, Donruss began what would become a long tradition of producing sports trading cards when the company released its first golf card and baseball card sets.

The company's venture into manufacturing golf cards was short-lived. The 1982 golf cards would be the last set that Donruss created. However, Donruss would continue to produce baseball cards for more than two decades.

With the exception of the 1999 and 2000 baseball seasons, Donruss produced baseball cards until the company ceased production of baseball cards after the 2005 baseball season.

One of the signature subsets in the base set of Donruss Baseball cards was the **Diamond Kings**, designed by the renowned sports artist **Dick Perez**.

In 1984, a corporate merger with international significance occurred. The Illinois-based Leaf Candy Company and Donruss were both purchased by a Finnish company, Huhtamaki Oy.

In 1985, the international flavour to the new company took on another aspect. That year Donruss produced a set of **Leaf** baseball cards for the Canadian market. Some collectors consider this set to be of more value than its American counterpart produced by Donruss. The reason for this thought is that the production numbers for the Canadians cards is considerably less than the American sports cards.

The Canadian product lasted for four years but the Leaf name did not disappear from the sports trading card industry. In 1990, Donruss produced a premium edition of baseball cards known as Leaf Baseball.

Collectors from that era will remember "the pack-buying frenzy" surrounding the release of this set. Perhaps recalling the rapid rise in prices of Upper Deck cards when they were first released in 1989, both collectors and dealers, placed a high value on some of the rookie and star cards in the 1990 Leaf Baseball set.

The company continued to increase its product line with another new set of baseball cards with the release of the Studio Baseball card set in 1991. This set was very unique to the early 1990s. For the first time in about three decades, black and white photographs of baseball players were available on the sports card market.

Donruss ventured further into the sports card industry with the release of Donruss and Leaf hockey card sets for the 1993-94 hockey season. The company continued to produce hockey cards until 2000.

In 1993, the company further broadened the scope of its sports card interests by entering the football card market. Donruss has continued to date to produce NFL cards under the banners of Donruss, Leaf and Playoff.

It would be hard for anyone to build a sports card collection of cards from the last quarter of a century without including some of the many fine sports card products created by Donruss.

Football Cards

The first football cards were produced in 1894. But it took more than half a century before the publication of football cards became an annual event for football card collectors.

In 1948 Bowman and Leaf both started issuing football cards. Since that date there has been at least one set of football cards released in the United States every year.

What is the Most Expensive Football Card?

If you guessed a sports card featuring a football superstar such as John Unitas, Joe Montana, Roger Staubach, Brett Favre or even Peyton Manning. You would be wrong.

The most expensive football card is one of John Dunlop.

Yes, John Dunlop! We think.

In 1894, what is believed to be the first set of football cards was released. They were known as the Mayo set and consisted of 35 cards of Ivy League football players. One card has an unidentified player. But, football card historians believe that the image on the card is that of John Dunlop of Harvard.

Less than a dozen of these cards are known to exist.

Goudey Sport Kings

It was almost 40 years before another issue of sports cards featuring football players. The 1933 Goudey Sport Kings featured football cards of gridiron legends Red Grange, Knute Rockne and Jim Thorpe.

National Chicle

Two years later, in 1935, the National Chicle set was released. This 36-card set is extremely rare. The set came in two series, 1-24 and 25-36. Some football collectors have told me that it is easier to find "a needle in a haystack" than to find a card from the second series!

If you do find a second series card from the 1935 National Chicle, the Bronco Nagurski Rookie Card is valued in excess of $8,000.00.

Bowman, Leaf and Topps

In 1948, Bowman and Leaf started producing football cards and two years later in 1950, Topps issued their first football card set.

Leaf ended its production of football cards after its 1949 football card set. After Bowman's last football set in 1955, football cards were almost exclusively, produced by Topps until 1989.

However, there were two short periods of time during the "Topps football era" that other companies released football card sets.

In 1960, Fleer printed its first of four consecutive football card sets. Fleer's football cards showcased the American

Football League. The last set produced by Fleer, the 1963 AFL set is a great set to collect, but difficult to find.

In 1964, the football card industry experienced a dramatic change. Topps took over the publication of the American Football League when the Philadelphia Gum company assumed the production rights to print the cards of the National Football League.

Topps became the sole manufacturer of football cards in 1968. Their dominance of the football card industry continued until 1989 when Action Packed, Pro Set and Score all kicked off their own football card sets.

In the 1990s, many other companies attempted to publish football cards during that period of the sports card collecting industry when there was an over-abundance of sports card sets released every year for every sport.

The wide selection and high quality of every football card product on the market today, makes this sport a great sports card-collecting commodity.

2001 Upper Deck Golf Card Set

The 2001 Upper Deck Golf card set could be called the "Tiger Woods Golf Card Set".

2001 Upper Deck Golf Set Review

Number of Cards in Set: 200

Hobby Favorite: #1 Tiger Woods Rookie Card

The 2001 Upper Deck Golf card set features a wide range of cards of golfers from every era of professional golf. For that reason, it is a great set of cards for both the casual and seasoned sports card collector.

Rookie Cards

The 2001 Upper Deck Golf card set is loaded with a fantastic selection of rookie cards. This golf set marked the first time in almost a decade that complete sets of licensed golf cards were produced. Therefore, the 2001 Upper Deck

Golf card set features rookie cards for golfers who were already PGA Tour veterans.

Rookie card collectors will love this set. After all, where else could you find a set of trading cards that boasts among its huge selection of rookie cards, the first cards of stars of the stature of Tiger Woods, Sergio Garcia, David Duval, Chris DiMarco, Adam Scott and Mike Weir?

Legends of Golf

If you love the tradition that surrounds the game of golf, then you are going to really appreciate the "Legends" cards that run from #53 Jack Nicklaus through to #68 Tom Weiskopf. The cards between these two all-time favourites include Arnold Palmer, Chi Chi Rodriguez and television commentator Gary McCord.

Young Guns

Perhaps, it is appropriate that the "Legends" card sequence gives way to a run of twenty cards featuring the next generation of golfers. The "Young Guns" entry in the set features the rookie cards of some of the younger golfers at that time on the PGA Tour including JJ Henry and Adam Scott.

Jack Nicklaus

While there are several cards of Tiger Woods in the set, including his rookie card, Upper Deck did not ignore the golfer that many consider the greatest of them all, Jack

Nicklaus. The 2001 Upper Deck set includes a multiple card feature about the "Golden Bear". Each card features a picture and story about a defining moment in Nicklaus' great golf career.

There are many other great theme-based sections in this 200-card set. The photography is Upper Deck's usually high quality. The stories on the back of the cards are interesting to read.

The choice of golfers for inclusion in the set is outstanding except for two omissions. Neither Vijay Singh nor Phil Mickelson is included in the set.

Insert Sets

Tiger's Tales: Ratio: 1 per pack

This 30-card set provides 30 different highlights from the golfing career of Tiger Woods. This is an easy to complete subset with some great photos of Tiger as a youngster.

The rest of the insert series in this set are much more difficult to find. The most difficult insert sets are probably the Player's Ink, the Tour Threads and Tour Gear cards and the hobby prices for these items tend to reflect the scarcity.

Despite the scarcity of some of the insert sets, the Upper Deck 2001 Golf set is a great collectible for hobbyists or fans of the game of golf.

About the Author

Paul White is a highly regarded sports historian who brings to life the exploits of the biggest names in the world of hockey with stories spanning the decades of the history of the National Hockey League. He has brought to the pages of books, magazines and the internet the hockey careers of many legendary Hall of Famers such as "Rocket" Richard and Jean Beliveau as well as the stars of today's hockey world such as Pittsburgh Penguin superstar Sidney Crosby and the New York Rangers' marquee player Brad Richards to his readers.

But Paul does not solely write about the stars of this great game. He has spent years collecting research about hockey players who seldom played on their team's power play or made an all-star team. After all, it takes more than a couple of star players to make a team. Every player from the 3rd and 4th lines to 6th and 7th defenseman has a story that should be told. How they made it to the bright lights of the NHL is often more interesting than the tale of the "Can't Miss" superstar!

Paul White is also known widely for his expertise in the world of sports card collecting. He was a confirmed hobbyist from the early years of his youth amassing a collection of hockey cards dating from the 1950s to date. For the last 25 years he has been active as a sports card vendor. White has owned or partnered in four sports card stores and in the intervening time he has been an active participant at sports card shows. In the pages of this book he will share with you his knowledge about sports cards to help you further enjoy this great hobby.

Paul White is a long-time member of SIHR (Society of International Hockey Research). White has written four books about hockey, and many magazine, newspaper and articles about the fastest game on ice. He has a passion for junior hockey and as a former goalie he just can't resist collecting unique hockey cards featuring goaltenders.

CPSIA information can be obtained
at www.ICGtesting.com
Printed in the USA
BVHW041459040422
633315BV00009B/928

9 781494 471026